# GREATEST MOVIE MONSTERS™

# GODZILLA

THERESE SHEA

rosen publishing's
rosen central®

Published in 2016 by The Rosen Publishing Group, Inc.
29 East 21st Street, New York, NY 10010

Copyright © 2016 by The Rosen Publishing Group, Inc.

First Edition

All rights reserved. No part of this book may be reproduced in any form without permission in writing from the publisher, except by a reviewer.

**Library of Congress Cataloging-in-Publication Data**

Shea, Therese.
Godzilla/Therese Shea.—First edition.
    pages cm.—(Greatest movie monsters)
Includes bibliographical references and index.
ISBN 978-1-4994-3533-7 (library bound)—ISBN 978-1-4994-3535-1 (pbk.)—ISBN 978-1-4994-3536-8 (6-pack)
1. Godzilla films—History and criticism—Juvenile literature. 2. Godzilla (Fictitious character)—Juvenile literature. I. Title.
PN1995.9.G63S54 2016
791.43'651—dc23

                                                                          2014045844

Manufactured in the United States of America

**On the cover:** When Gareth Edwards' *Godzilla* hit theaters in Japan in the summer of 2014, the city of Tokyo unveiled this 21.7-foot (6.6-meter) model of the movie's monster. At night, the monster would "come to life" during a light show, breathing mist and roaring at audiences.

# CONTENTS

**1** GODZILLA AWAKENS ...................... 4

**2** INVENTING GODZILLA ..................... 12

**3** A MAJOR MON-STAR ...................... 22

**4** THE GODZILLA PHENOMENON ........ 31

FILMOGRAPHY .......................... 40

GLOSSARY ................................. 42

FOR MORE INFORMATION ......... 43

FOR FURTHER READING ............ 45

BIBLIOGRAPHY ......................... 46

INDEX ........................................ 47

# CHAPTER 1

# GODZILLA AWAKENS

Huge spikes poke through the ocean's surface. A whole, scaly body emerges, pushing aside water, which causes tsunamilike waves. A giant reptilian creature reaches the shore, stands on two feet, and lumbers toward the city to the horror of the people scrambling to get out of the way for fear of getting crushed. Godzilla has awoken!

Whether you think of Godzilla as terrifying or campy, you know of the famous monster—even if you have never seen any of his movies. The dinosaurlike animal walks on two legs, somewhat like a *Tyrannosaurus rex*, but with two muscular arms and a tail that can take down several skyscrapers with a single swipe. Something about this fictional creature has fascinated people for decades, resulting in multiple versions of the beast throughout many, many movies.

There is more than meets the eye when it comes to Godzilla. Certainly, moviegoers watch the various films

# GODZILLA AWAKENS

*The Godzilla movies' unique mixture of realism and fantasy has held audiences spellbound for decades.*

for different reasons: They want to be scared of something that could not possibly harm them in real life. They want to laugh at the costumes and scenery. They want to imagine that such a fearsome creature might exist in the depths of the oceans. Perhaps the reason why Godzilla has such longevity in popular culture is that he can fulfill these many desires for so many people.

# GODZILLA

## ATTACK OF THE MOVIE MONSTERS

The first Godzilla movie, the Japanese-made *Gojira*, was released in 1954. This was a time when monster films were filling the seats of theaters. *King Kong*, a 1933 production, had been rereleased and was very popular. *The Beast from 20,000 Fathoms* had been released in 1953 to great excitement, too. Adding to its appeal in Japan, *Gojira* was the first Japanese monster movie ever.

At first look, it may seem that Godzilla is just another movie monster, only meant to thrill the audience. But there had long been a place in Japanese folklore for such a monster. Fantasy creatures such as dragons were often featured in Japanese myths and legends. Godzilla possesses some dragonlike qualities. Like them, he attacks only when mistreated. Otherwise, Godzilla is a creature that disregards or even acts with goodwill toward people.

Equally as significant in the consciousness of the Japanese people was a reverence and fear of nature. Because of its location, Japan has been subject to earthquakes, tsunamis, and other natural disasters. The disasters often strike so quickly and violently that years ago it might have seemed easier to believe that a supernatural creature was at work rather than Earth's geologic activity. A creature that embodies these disasters and inflicts similar destruction and chaos is a fitting representation of this awesome power of nature.

However, further study of the backstory of the movie reveals the figure of Godzilla and particularly his debut movie

# GODZILLA AWAKENS

is perhaps more of a reflection of that time in world history than Japan's ancient culture. Godzilla, though his form is certainly sprung from imagination and mythology, was also born out of fear of nuclear radiation and atomic weaponry.

## THE *LUCKY DRAGON* INCIDENT

On March 1, 1954, the United States tested a hydrogen bomb on Bikini Atoll. The scientists responsible for the bomb were

*The Japanese fishing boat the* Lucky Dragon, *which was caught up in the aftermath of nuclear testing, is shown here about two weeks after the nuclear blast. Its chief radio operator died six months later.*

gravely mistaken about the size of its impact. It turned out to be one thousand times more powerful than either of the bombs dropped on Hiroshima or Nagasaki, Japan, during World War II. It created a crater 1 mile (1.6 kilometers) wide.

About an hour and half later, the Japanese fishing boat *Lucky Dragon*, about 80 miles (129 km) away from the test site, was rained on by a strange ashlike substance, which turned out to be radioactive. The crew fell deathly ill, with one man on board dying. Nearby Marshall Island also experienced the ash rain. Many reported burns and loss of hair before they were rescued.

Reports of previous bomb testing and fallout from the bombs dropped on Nagasaki and Hiroshima had not been permitted in the press. There was concern that the horrific effects of radiation poisoning resulting from the bombs would cause anti-American feelings during a time when the world was recovering from war. The United States occupied Japan until 1952, so keeping newspapers and other media sources from reporting was not hard.

But after the *Lucky Dragon* incident, Japanese newspapers printed the account and demanded answers. One headline pleaded: "Tell us the truth about the ashes of death." As a result, millions of Japanese refused to eat fish, fearing they would share the fate of the Marshall Islanders and *Lucky Dragon* fishermen if they ate from the same waters. Additionally, the Japanese people wanted an end to nuclear testing. Though the United States would

## HIBAKUSHA

*Hibakusha* means "bomb-affected people" in Japanese. This is an official status in Japan, created so that the people affected by the dropped bombs on Hiroshima and Nagasaki would receive Japanese government assistance. Many of these people were severely burned or later became ill of cancers such as leukemia. Sadly, because little was known about radiation in the 1940s, even those whose health was not impaired were excluded from society by those afraid of being infected by radiation through them. *Hibakusha* could not get jobs and often could not marry. According to the United Nations Office of Disarmament Affairs, there were more than 420,000 *hibakusha*, including 269,446 in Hiroshima and 152,276 in Nagasaki. While most are Japanese, several thousand victims were from other parts of the globe. Many of those who survived worked toward ending nuclear armament by sharing their stories.

later admit its mistake and pay restitution to the people affected, it was an anxious time for the Japanese.

## AWAKENING THE BEAST

Today, quite a few people think of Godzilla films as "cheesy B-movies," even if they are fans. And it is hard to argue that many of the original movie sequels are not. However, the first Godzilla film, *Gojira*, was actually considered to be quite shocking to audiences at the time. Although the special

# GODZILLA

effects and costumes were basic and simple compared to modern movie special effects, during that film era they were very effective—even frightening.

In the original movie, Godzilla is awakened by nuclear testing. In his anger, he tries to destroy the city of Tokyo. Godzilla's destructive actions are a direct result of humankind's increasingly destructive weapons. By the movie's end, viewers realize that Godzilla also represents the fear that humanity will one day destroy itself through its actions. Many people who have

*This image shows the city of Hiroshima, Japan, after an atomic bomb was dropped on it in August 1945. The area was devastated by the nuclear weapon.*

studied *Gojira* agree, pointing out that it is less about the devastation wrought by the monster and more about the fear of the Japanese people.

The destruction of their cities and homes was something that the Japanese had already experienced during World War II (1939–1945). They also feared nuclear fallout in their daily lives following the war. These were the issues at the forefront of Japanese culture and were mirrored and addressed in the first movie. Though some point out that Godzilla is descended from other movie monsters of the day, the heavy issues explored in the movie that features him make it something unique, a standout among other monster movies.

At the same time, interestingly, the movie was accepted and enjoyed as entertainment by cultures that did not harbor the same concerns as the Japanese. And, even as time moved on and the issues facing the Japanese people changed, Godzilla endured as a popular movie monster. Incredibly, considering its legacy, the movie was made almost by accident, as an afterthought. *Gojira*, the film that spawned the long-lived movie series, was put into production only to fill an empty slot in a movie studio's schedule.

# CHAPTER 2

# INVENTING GODZILLA

Tomoyuki Tanaka was a producer at the Tōhō movie studios in Tokyo, Japan. At the beginning of 1954, Tanaka found himself panicked. The Indonesian government would not allow Japanese actors into their country. And a movie that was being made by both Japanese and Indonesian movie studios was abruptly cancelled. That meant Tōhō would not have the expected film to release in the fall of that year. Tōhō, once a hit-making studio, desperately needed a successful film to stay afloat financially after falling on hard times following World War II.

Tanaka scoured his brain for an idea. He was a fan of monster movies and had just read about the movie *The Beast from 20,000 Fathoms*. The story goes that, as he sat in an airplane flying over the Pacific Ocean, he first conceived of a monster that came from the Pacific fathoms. He wondered if Tōhō could make a movie similar to *The Beast from 20,000 Fathoms* but explore deeper issues haunting the Japanese people, including

# INVENTING GODZILLA

*Producer Tomoyuki Tanaka poses next to two replicas of his most famous creation, known to American audiences as Godzilla.*

the fear of nuclear weapons. Tanaka hired Eiji Tsuburaya for special effects and Ishiro Honda to direct the film.

## TANAKA'S TEAM

Eiji Tsuburaya had a gift for mechanics. He built his own camera as a child. He was also an expert at making models for Japanese wartime propaganda films, some so realistic that American forces thought they were real places on film. For

# GODZILLA

this new Tōhō film, Tsuburaya was asked to create a model of Tokyo that would be "destroyed" by the monster in the movie (which monster-movie fan Tsuburaya hoped would be a giant octopus).

Director Ishiro Honda had personally encountered the devastation of World War II. As a Japanese soldier, he survived the bombing of Tokyo and witnessed the aftermath of the atomic bombs. According to the newspaper the *Telegraph*, he said of the experiences, "There was a feeling that the world was already

**Director Ishiro Honda (left) examines a Godzilla model on the set of one of his many films.**

coming to an end. Ever since I felt that this atomic fear would hang around our necks for ever." Honda was eager to explore these feelings in the film and hired screenwriter Takeo Murata to incorporate them into the script.

The draft of the script was first called *Big Monster from 20,000 Miles Beneath the Sea*. Since that sounded much too close to the American movie that influenced it, *The Beast from 20,000 Fathoms*, the name was changed to *Gojira*. The origins of this name are not known, though it is a combination of two Japanese words: *gorira* (gorilla) and *kujira* (whale). These animals do not reflect the shape of the monster, a dinosaurlike creature, but they do suggest its size and ferocity. The name would later become "Godzilla" to American audiences because that is the pronunciation of the Japanese word *gojira*.

## THE MAKING OF THE MONSTER

Eiji Tsuburaya created the iconic Godzilla suit, too. His final design gave the monster a spiky back and tail and a sort of bumpy-looking hide. Some think it was meant to suggest that Godzilla was burned by nuclear blasts. (A discarded design had even given Godzilla a mushroom-shaped head, inspired by the mushroom clouds released by atomic bombs.)

It was very difficult making a suit that looked realistic but was still flexible enough for an actor to move inside. Three cables came out of the back of the costume; two were for the operation of the eyes and one moved the mouth. Actor

# GODZILLA

Haruo Nakajima takes a break during the filming of one of the many movies in which he starred as Godzilla. He needed to stay hydrated in the sweat-inducing suit!

and judo expert Haruo Nakajima donned the suit in the film. Weighing 220 pounds (100 kilograms), the latex and bamboo suit was so hot that he could not spend more than two minutes in it or walk more than 30 feet (9 meters). Cups of sweat collected within the legs. Nakajima often fainted in the suit!

The newest way of "animating" a creature on film at that time was stop-motion. In this technique, an object is moved in small amounts between photographed frames, creating the illusion of movement when the frames are played as a sequence.

# INVENTING GODZILLA

Eiji Tsuburaya, however, invented "suitmation." The monster movement was shot at double speed and later slowed to create a great stomping effect. By today's standards, the results might still seem like a man in a costume. However, for audiences then, "it made you believe it was really happening," according to famed science fiction director Steven Spielberg in David Kalat's *A Critical History and Filmography of Tōhō's Godzilla Series*.

To provide Godzilla's sound effects, Japanese composer Akira Ifukube was brought on board. He created music that reflected the doom that accompanied the monster. He also created the noise of Godzilla's footsteps and roar. He made the roar by rubbing a leather glove across the strings of a double bass. The thundering footsteps, too, were created with the double bass in addition to an electronic echo.

The use of a miniature Tokyo helped maintain the idea of Godzilla as a huge monster. All scenes with real actors were filmed separately. In fact, this movie style later inspired special-effects wizard and *Star Wars* creator George Lucas to use miniature models in his film series. There are some "goofs" that appear, such as wires attached to planes buzzing around Godzilla's head. Scenes of Godzilla underwater were filmed with an aquarium of fish placed between the camera and the monster.

In all, Tsuburaya's special effects were about one-third of the film's entire budget. *Gojira* became the most expensive film

# GODZILLA

## IS GODZILLA A GIRL OR BOY?

Though Godzilla has been around for nearly sixty years, people still debate about whether the monster is a boy or girl. In some later movies, Godzilla has offspring, making people think the creature is a female. Some of these movies are not well respected in the franchise, however, and many fans choose to disregard what they have to say about the monster. A character in one of the movies (*Godzilla*, 1998) suggests that Godzilla can reproduce by itself; it does not need to be either male or female to do so. Additionally, Godzilla is often referred to in movies as a "he." In this volume, the monster will be referred to similarly.

ever made in Japan. In fact, it was ten times more expensive than the average Japanese film.

## HOW IT UNFOLDS

The opening scene of *Gojira* was in honor of the *Lucky Dragon* boat incident. A crew aboard a fishing boat sees a bright flash of light—a nuclear bomb. However, unlike in real life, the boat in the movie catches fire and sinks. The bomb awakens Godzilla. "Mankind had created the bomb," producer Tomoyuki Tanaka later commented, "and now nature [in the form of Godzilla] was going to take revenge on mankind."

Godzilla himself is like a bomb. Director Ishiro Honda said, "I took the characteristics of an atomic bomb and applied them to [the monster]." Besides its massive size and destruc-

# INVENTING GODZILLA

tive tail, Godzilla had the power of "thermonuclear breath." This was demonstrated by tiny towers of wax being melted by a heat source off camera. The aftermath of Tokyo's destruction mirrored the imagery of World War II: panicked crowds, buildings reduced to rubble, hospitals filled with the wounded, and children separated from parents. While Godzilla caused the wreckage this time, the horrific effects were the same—and the atomic bomb was the cause of his fury.

However, much of the movie consists of characters debating over what to do about Godzilla. Should they study him? Should they kill him? And how would this even be possible? The military tries to electrocute him and fires missiles at him but to no effect. He easily swats away weapons and planes.

However, a young scientist develops a terrible new weapon, something he calls an "oxygen destroyer." Put simply, it removes all oxygen from an area of water, reducing any creatures in it to dust. When this weapon is discovered, the scientist refuses to let anyone use it. He does not want it to be reproduced because he thought nations could destroy other nations with it. However, after he sees the mass destruction Godzilla wreaked on Tokyo, he consents that it should be used just this once. He destroys the plans so the oxygen destroyer can never be made again. The scientist then sacrifices himself while exploding the bomb in the water near the sleeping Godzilla. The weapon works, but the jubilation over the death of the monster is tempered by the death of the scientist and the realization of how lethal the weapon really was.

# GODZILLA

This is the poster for the Gojira movie released in Japan in 1954. The artwork spotlights the creature's size and thermonuclear breath.

# INVENTING GODZILLA

In the final scene in the movie, another scientist muses whether other Godzilla monsters exist. He then remarks: "If we keep conducting nuclear tests, another [Godzilla] may appear somewhere in the world." One more time, the audience is reminded of the dangers of nuclear technology.

## RECEPTION

It was these constant reminders of the real message of the movie that divided audiences. They had already lived through seeing their cities destroyed in real life. Some did not care to see them destroyed again, even if by a fictional monster on screen. Yet, audiences still flocked to the theaters—such a spectacle had to be seen. And rather than laughing at the rubber-suited monster, many felt a sympathy for the creature that had been scarred by the atomic bomb, just as some of them had been. To them, Godzilla seemed a victim of the new technology rather than an enemy.

*Gojira* was nominated for the Japanese Movie Association's Best Picture; it would be the only Godzilla movie to be nominated for this award. Though it lost to the famous classic *Seven Samurai*, it did win Best Visual Effects.

*Gojira* was so popular that plans began to distribute the film to Western audiences. The Godzilla monster was about to take over the world—with some slight changes to the movie.

# CHAPTER 3

# A MAJOR MON-STAR

In 1956, American Joseph E. Levine bought the rights to release *Gojira* in the United States. He dubbed and edited the film and retitled it *Godzilla, King of the Monsters!* In all, Levine cut forty minutes from the original movie, including references to bomb-affected Nagasaki, food contaminated by nuclear testing, and wartime bomb shelters. *Gojira* was scrubbed of most references to nuclear danger, and there was little to remind audiences of the part that the United States played in the nuclear activities in and around Japan.

The new material added made the movie seem more like an American film, including scenes with actor Raymond Burr as a reporter in the city of Tokyo. The result was closer to the stereotypical monster movie than the original. It was purely for thrills.

Critics were not pleased. *New York Times* film reviewer Bosley Crowther scathingly called it "an incredibly awful film." Another critic complained of the production quality, saying

## A MAJOR MON-STAR

that Godzilla looked like he was made of rubber and the set used "about $20 worth of toy trains."

However, movie posters enticed audiences, promising a "psychotic cavalcade of electrifying horror." Audiences filled the seats, again and again. The film was so popular, in fact, that it was rereleased in Japan with subtitles!

## *KAIJU*

The popularity of both versions of the first Godzilla movie meant that the Tōhō production company began making more. These proved to be less serious than the initial offering. A genre of movies called *kaiju* ("monster") movies began in Japan. Tōhō developed many *kaiju* after Godzilla, some of which costarred with Godzilla in his movies to battle or befriend him, sometimes both. These included:

**Mothra:** She is a giant moth who costarred in eleven Godzilla movies in all, the first in 1964, *Mothra vs. Godzilla*. She usually acts on behalf of humans.

**King Ghidorah:** Introduced in 1964's *Ghidorah, the Three-Headed Monster*, he is a three-headed dragon monster with two tails who is able to shoot lightning from his mouth and create earthquakes with batlike wings.

**Rodan:** This giant radioactive flying reptile first helps Godzilla beat King Ghidorah in *Ghidorah, the Three-Headed Monster*.

# GODZILLA

*Godzilla is shown along with Ghidorah (upper left) and Rodan (upper right) in this scene from the 1965 film,* Invasion of Astro-Monster *(or* Monster Zero [1970] *in the United States).*

**Minilla:** A small, plump version of Godzilla, he first appeared in 1967's *Son of Godzilla*. Minilla hatched from an egg and is a friend to humans.

**Hedorah**: He is an alien smog monster who feeds on Earth's pollution in 1971's *Godzilla vs. Hedorah*, growing bigger, stronger, and more deadly.

**Gigan**: First appearing in 1972's *Godzilla vs. Gigan*, Gigan is an alien monster that is part robot, with a circular-saw torso and hooks for hands and feet.

**MechaGodzilla**: First appearing in 1974's *Godzilla vs. MechaGodzilla*, this robot version of Godzilla was created by aliens who conspired to take over Earth.

# A MAJOR MON-STAR

## GODZILLA VS. KING KONG

Godzilla went head to head with another famous movie monster, and one that inspired his creation, King Kong. *King Kong vs. Godzilla* was released in 1962. It was a box office smash, selling more tickets than any other Godzilla movie to date. Many looked forward to the matchup between the huge American ape and the enormous Japanese reptile. Tōhō studios

*Both Godzilla and King Kong would wreak destruction in the film that bore both of their names. The film's finale features an underwater battle.*

## ERAS OF GODZILLA

In all, Tōhō produced twenty-eight Godzilla movies from 1954 to 2004 with varying degrees of box-office success. The focus changed from serious themes to outlandish monsters and cartoonish violence and then back again. Generally, Godzilla experts separate the *kaiju* films into different eras.

The Shōwa series of films, numbering fifteen in all, began with *Gojira* in 1954 and ended around 1975 with the release of *Terror of MechaGodzilla*. The era was named for Japan's Shōwa emperor, Hirohito. With a few exceptions, including the first movie, these films were a mixture of light-heartedness and destruction. Godzilla began to turn into a friendlier monster in this era. William Tsutsui explained in the *Telegraph* that the series reflects Japanese society: in the 1960s and 1970s, Japan's economy was doing well, the Japanese people were happier, and so Godzilla was not Japan's enemy but its protector, a happier monster than in 1954, who took on more human characteristics. Additionally, by the 1970s, the films were being made primarily for a very young audience, who demanded lots of monsters and action sequences over plot and substance. Shrinking film budgets and Tōhō's insistence on using physical effects rather than more sophisticated effects resulted in the films looking increasingly campy next to other movies of the same genre. Eventually, low ticket sales forced Tōhō to stop making Godzilla films for a number of years.

# A MAJOR MON-STAR

The Heisei era of films (after the Heisei emperor Akihito) lasted from 1984's *The Return of Godzilla* to 1995's *Godzilla vs. Destoroyah*. (Experts note that *Gojira* is a part of the Heisei era, too, as *The Return of Godzilla* is a sequel to *Gojira*.) The seven movies of this series had the big budgets and computer-generated graphics that the previous films lacked. Additionally, they were darker movies highlighting more serious issues such as the morality of manipulating genetics and the effects of pollution on the environment. Though each of the Heisei films did well at the box office, many fans discovered they missed the humor, nonsensical plots, and even low-tech quality of the Shōwa films. In an effort to bring in bigger audiences, Tōhō decided to show the death of Godzilla in *Godzilla vs. Destoroyah*. This may have been done to conclude the continuing narrative that ran throughout these movies as well as to clear the way for the 1998 American movie *Godzilla* and its new plot, which would be released in Japan, too.

However, this American movie was so disliked by audiences that Tōhō revived Godzilla again. The Millenium, or Shinsei, era began in 1999 with *Godzilla 2000: Millennium*. Each of the six films of this era was like a sequel to the original *Gojira*, giving the audience an alternative history to the creature and his exploits. This Godzilla was a return to the creature as an angry destroyer of cities. Generally, the Shinsei films were well received by Godzilla fans but still performed disappointingly at the box office. Reasons for this are unclear; some blame a shift in the interests of the popular culture, especially a youth market more interested in anime, a style of Japanese animation.

# GODZILLA

## GODZILLA AND FUKUSHIMA

Following an earthquake in Japan on March 11, 2011, tsunami waves damaged the Fukushima Daiichi nuclear plant in northern Japan. Now called one of the worst nuclear accidents in history, so much radiation leaked into the surrounding area that it likely will not be habitable for decades. According to William Tsutsui, fears of radiation following the Fukushima meltdown caused a spike in Google searches of Godzilla. In the *Telegraph*, Tsutsui said, "People went back to look at the movies, and look at the lessons filmmakers had been bringing forward about the fears of untrammelled nuclear energy and weapons testing." Toshio Takahashi, a literature professor at Tokyo's Waseda University, thinks Godzilla is more about making people ask questions about their actions. In a Reuters article, he said, "If Godzilla appeared (in Japan) now, he'd ultimately force people to ask themselves hard questions about Fukushima."

*An aerial photograph shows the Fukushima Daiichi plant three days after an earthquake and tsunami damaged it beyond repair.*

Tōhō expected Godzilla fans would rally for a fiftieth anniversary film, *Godzilla: Final Wars*. Released in 2004, it was the most expensive Godzilla movie to date. Disappointingly, the film was considered a box-office failure, causing Tōhō to refuse to license Godzilla to other countries' studios or make anymore Godzilla movies of their own for a decade.

## THE AMERICAN FILMS

There have been five American Godzilla movies after 1956's *Godzilla, King of the Monsters!* Two were similar to that one in that they were originally Japanese movies but were dubbed and provided with footage of American actors. These were *King Kong vs. Godzilla* (1963) and *Godzilla 1985* (1985). In 1970, *Monster Zero*, a coproduction between Tōhō and American studio UPA, was released.

However, two other films were entirely produced by U.S. studios. *Godzilla*, released in 1998, was widely panned by critics and fans. They lamented the acting, directing, and the plot that reinvented the Godzilla origin story: radiation turns a lizard into a gigantic creature that lays eggs in New York City. Still, the movie was successful at the box office—and successful in spurring Tōhō to "redeem" Godzilla through new films.

In contrast, 2014's *Godzilla* was much better received. In it, Godzilla, a creature whose origins are unknown, suddenly appears to save Earth's people from destruction at the hands of *kaiju* that they have awoken. The film was set after the meltdown

# GODZILLA

*The monster in the 2014* Godzilla *resembles the Godzilla of original Japanese movies, including its famous thermonuclear breath.*

of the Fukushima Daiichi nuclear plant. The terror of this actual event is addressed in the film. As in the original *Gojira*, people's real fears of the effects of nuclear power and radiation are explored seriously in the context of a monster movie. This *Godzilla* proved so successful that sequels are planned. Some have even named a new era of Godzilla movies "the Legendary era" after the Legendary company that produces them. Time will tell how long this era will last or whether there will be another.

s, producers, and screenwrit- works' existence. *Cloverfield*, people the sort of thrill I had ," said producer J. J. Abrams monster, an angry underwater offers the audience thrills and plorations of social fears and

**Cloverfield (2008) presents much of the action through a character's video camera. However, the film featured some spectacular special effects.**

# CHAPTER

# THE G(
# PHEN(

Godzilla films are revered by fa
mainstream movie audiences.
in several movies only to return in the
because it made sense to the character's
not—but because the public wanted more.

In Japan, that appreciation for Godzilla
with nostalgia for a fictional creature that, alt
and destructive in some movies, is still considered
treasure—and perhaps one of Japan's most fam
instantly recognizable exports. In the United State
other Western countries, the demand for Godzilla st
from a renewed interest in the monster movie genre i
recent years. The new Godzilla may be a Hollywood
remake of a classic monster, but the most current computer-
generated graphics have yielded breathtaking results.

# THE GODZILLA PHENOMENON

issues"—a combination similar to the original *Gojira* and other classic Tōhō *kaiju* films. When critics asked Abrams about his decision to set his movie in New York City despite the lingering fears and memories of the September 11 terrorist attacks, he referenced Godzilla's setting in Tokyo just a few years after World War II: "It must have had a similar feeling. It was very much a way to deal, in a social, communal way, with everyone's common fears."

In 2013, director Guillermo del Toro freely admitted to drawing inspiration from Japanese monster movies. "I grew up in the 1960s, the decade when the *kaiju* genre was at its peak," Del Toro told EFE news service. "Now those films are seen with humor or nostalgia and in *Pacific Rim* I wanted to provide a fresh and spectacular look at those . . . mythologies for a new generation." For his movie's *kaiju*, del Toro chose a reptile and a crablike monster that emerge from beneath Earth's crust. Del Toro has acknowledged he loves the idea of his creatures meeting up with Godzilla in a possible future sequel.

## STEPPING OFF THE BIG SCREEN

Because of Godzilla's success in the movies, he has stomped his way into other genres of media as well. Godzilla has starred in two different animated series. In 1978, Tōhō and Hanna-Barbera Productions created a *Godzilla* cartoon, which aired both in the United States and Japan for twenty-six episodes until 1981. Godzilla functioned as a hero in this show, called on to help a team of scientists when needed.

# GODZILLA

## COULD GODZILLA EXIST?

Godzilla is a fictional character, but like Bigfoot and the Loch Ness Monster, some might wonder if such a creature really could live in our world. Could a gigantic reptile exist, even if it could hide from civilization simply by sleeping in the depths of the ocean? Scientists have actually commented on that. Though Godzilla's size has changed much throughout the years, according to an article in *Popular Mechanics* online, in the most recent *Godzilla* (2014), he is about 30 stories tall, or about 325 feet (99 meters) tall. He probably weighs about 164,000 tons (149,000 metric tons). His bones would have to be stronger than any known animal bones to support that body, and he would need to eat constantly to have energy to move. Even so, scientists think an animal that big would simply overheat and its organs would explode. The heaviest land animal was a dinosaur called *Argentinosaurus*. It was "only" 100 tons (90 metric tons), 70 feet (20 m) tall, and 115 feet (35 m) long.

This may be what Argentinosaurus looked like. This huge animal was much smaller than Godzilla is supposed to be.

# THE GODZILLA PHENOMENON

After the American *Godzilla* came out in 1998, the animated *Godzilla: The Series* picked up where that storyline left off, running for forty episodes from 1998 to 2000. In it, a team of human heroes is helped by the son of Godzilla in defeating various *kaiju* who wreak havoc on the world. (The series was actually better received by Godzilla fans than the 1998 movie.)

Godzilla comic books, or manga as they are called in Japan, have been produced since *Gojira* hit the screen in 1954. Many of these were retellings of the movies. However, there were original stories as well. Both Marvel Comics and Dark Horse Comics, two American publishing houses, have produced Godzilla comic series, too. Legendary Comics, an offshoot of the Legendary Pictures that produced the 2014 *Godzilla* movie, published a prequel graphic novel called *Godzilla: Awakening*. It was a *New York Times* best seller.

Since 1983, many, many Godzilla video games have been produced for a variety of computer and game systems, including the Nintendo Entertainment System, Wii, and PS3. Some of these games used *kaiju* from the movies while others introduced completely new characters.

There are Godzilla rings, necklaces, and earrings, too! In fact, in 2014, one jeweler made a solid-gold figurine of the creature that weighed 33 pounds (15 kg) and is thought to be worth $1.47 million.

There is so much Godzilla merchandise—playing cards, key chains, action figures, board games, candy dispensers, puppets, T-shirts, and more—that Godzilla's name and figure

# GODZILLA

Godzilla is so widespread throughout Japanese culture that even children embrace figures of the creature, once thought to be a horrific monster.

are known even by people who have not seen the movies. Japanese toy stores sell plush Godzillas that children treat affectionately as teddy bears. The unofficial monster of Japan, even with its startlingly serious origins, is cuddled with pride.

## GODZILLA GET-TOGETHERS

Unsurprisingly, Godzilla fans do not only want more Godzilla movies, media, and merchandise, they want to connect with other Godzilla fans. Godzilla fan clubs and appreciation sites can be found online through Facebook, Google+, and other Internet meeting places.

For those who want to meet up in person, there is G-Fest, an annual summer convention dedicated to the *kaiju* genre. Fans watch film screenings, meet the people in and behind the scenes of the movies, attend presentations, and have the opportunity to purchase merchandise. Attendance has been increasing in recent years. More than three thousand attended the eleventh G-Fest in Chicago, Illinois, in 2014.

G-Fest is orchestrated by Daikaiju Enterprises (DKE), the organization that is also the publisher of *G-FAN* magazine. This is the world's only magazine dedicated to giant movie monsters, in particular Japanese *kaiju*. DKE also runs G-Fan.com, an Internet source with resources of much interest to Godzilla fans. There are links to Godzilla stories written by fans and even information about how to join a Godzilla tour of Japan, including Tōhō studios.

# GODZILLA

*Haruo Nakajima (left) the actor who first filled the Godzilla suit in the original movies appears at the 2014 Fear FestEvil, which celebrates horror and other types of pop culture.*

## LEGACY

With each new reincarnation of Godzilla, the question of why the monster has such an enduring image arises. Few movie monsters have persisted so long in popular culture. Certainly, no others have been featured in so many films. Even after box office numbers seemed to reflect that the public needed a break from Godzilla, revivals have proved

# THE GODZILLA PHENOMENON

successful, showing that the monster has something for new audiences and new generations.

Godzilla's popularity is of a complex nature. He means different things to different people. He reminds them of their youth, of watching Godzilla movies in the theaters or at home. Some people enjoy the comic side of Godzilla, as portrayed by a man in a rubber suit walking through miniature sets. Others prefer Godzilla as a destructive monster but enjoy that he is a far cry from the gross and terrifying horror movies of today. Still others love Godzilla the hero, saving the world no matter what weird and evil villain he faces. Something about Godzilla appeals to the imagination, even if the source of that appeal varies from person to person.

As more Godzilla movies are now in production, it appears he will be around for a significant time to come. Godzilla was born in post war Japan, a reflection of the consequences of conflict and nuclear weapons. Yet somehow, he transformed into a creature that could reflect the issues of many eras and many cultures while maintaining the image of an always entertaining movie monster.

# FILMOGRAPHY

***Gojira* (1954) (international title:** *Godzilla, King of the Monsters!* **[1956])**
Director: Ishiro Honda
Actors: Akira Takarada, Momoko Kochi and Haruo Nakajima

***Godzilla Raids Again* (1955)**
Director: Motoyoshi Oda
Actors: Hiroshi Koizumi, Takashi Shimura, and Haruo Nakajima

***King Kong vs. Godzilla* (1962)**
Director: Ishiro Honda
Actors: Kenji Sahara, Haruo Nakajima, and Ichiro Arishima

***Godzilla vs. Mothra* (1964)**
Director: Ishiro Honda
Actors: Akira Takarada, Hiroshi Koizumi, and Haruo Nakajima

***Ghidorah, the Three-Headed Monster* (1964)**
Director: Ishiro Honda
Actors: Akiko Wakabayashi, Hiroshi Koizumi, and Haruo Nakajima

***Invasion of Astro-Monster*** **(*Godzilla vs. Monster Zero*) (1965)**
Director: Ishiro Honda
Actors: Nick Adams, Akira Takarada, and Haruo Nakajima.

***Ebirah, Horror of the Deep*** **(*Godzilla vs. the Sea Monster*) (1966)**
Director: Jun Fukuda
Actors: Akira Takarada, Kumi Mizuno, and Haruo Nakajima

***Son of Godzilla* (1967)**
Director: Jun Fukuda
Actors: Tadao Takashima, Akihiko Hirata, and Haruo Nakajima

***Destroy All Monsters* (1968)**
Directors: Ishiro Honda
Actors: Akira Kubo, Jun Tazaki, and Haruo Nakajima.

***Godzilla's Revenge* (1969)**
Director: Ishiro Honda
Actors: Tomonori Yazaki, Hideyo Amamoto, and Haruo Nakajima

***Godzilla vs. Hedorah*** **(*Godzilla vs. the Smog Monster*) (1971)**
Director: Yoshimitsu Banno
Actors: Akira Yamauchi, Hiroyuki Kawase, and Haruo Nakajima

***Godzilla vs. Gigan* (1972)**
Director: Jun Fukuda
Actors: Hiroshi Ishikawa, Yuriko Hishimi, and Haruo Nakajima

***Godzilla vs. Megalon* (1973)**
Director: Jun Fukuda
Actors: Katsuhiko Sasaki, Hiroyuki Kawase, and Shinji Takagi

***Godzilla vs. MechaGodzilla* (1974)**
Director: Jun Fukuda
Actors: Akihiko Hirata, Hiroshi Koizumi, and Isao Zushi

***Terror of MechaGodzilla* (1975)**
Director: Ishiro Honda
Actors: Katsuhiko Sasaki, Tomoko Ai, and Toru Kawai

**The Return of Godzilla (Godzilla 1985) (1984)**
Director: Koji Hashimoto
Actors: Ken Tanaka, Raymond Burr, and Kenpachiro Satsuma

**Godzilla vs. Biollante (1989)**
Director: Kazuki Ohmori.
Actors: Kunihiko Mitamura, Yoshiko Tanaka, and Kenpachiro Satsuma

**Godzilla vs. King Ghidorah (1991)**
Director: Kazuki Ohmori.
Actors: Kosuke Toyohara, Anna Nakagawa, and Kenpachiro Satsuma

**Godzilla vs. Mothra (Godzilla & Mothra: The Battle for Earth) (1992)**
Director: Takao Okawara
Actors: Tetsuya Bessho, Satomi Kobayashi, and Kenpachiro Satsuma

**Godzilla vs. MechaGodzilla 2 (1993)**
Director: Takao Okawara.
Actors: Masahiro Takashima, Kenji Sahara, and Kenpachiro Satsuma

**Godzilla vs. SpaceGodzilla (1994)**
Director: Kensho Yamashita.
Actors: Megumi Odaka, Jun Hashizume, and Kenpachiro Satsuma

**Godzilla vs. Destoroyah (1995)**
Director: Takao Okawara.
Actors: Takuro Tatsumi, Yoko Ishino, and Kenpachiro Satsuma

**Godzilla (1998)**
Director: Roland Emmerich.
Actors: Matthew Broderick, Jean Reno, and Hank Azaria

**Godzilla 2000: Millennium (Godzilla 2000) (1999)**
Director: Takao Okawara
Actors: Takehiro Murata, Hiroshi Abe, and Tsutomu Kitagawa

**Godzilla vs. Megaguirus (2000)**
Director: Masaaki Tezuka
Actors: Misato Tanaka, Shosuke Tanihara, and Tsutomu Kitagawa

**Godzilla, Mothra & King Ghidorah: Giant Monsters All-Out Attack (2001)**
Director: Shusuke Kaneko
Actors: Chiharu Niiyama, Ryudo Uzaki, and Mizuho Yoshida

**Godzilla Against MechaGodzilla (2002)**
Director: Masaaki Tezuka
Actors: Yumiko Shaku, Shin Takuma, and Tsutomu Kitagawa

**Godzilla: Tokyo S.O.S. (2003)**
Director: Masaaki Tezuka
Actors: Noboru Kaneko, Miho Yoshioka, and Tsutomu Kitagawa

**Godzilla: Final Wars (2004)**
Director: Ryuhei Kitamura
Actors: Masahiro Matsuoka, Rei Kikukawa, and Tsutomu Kitagawa

**Godzilla (2014)**
Director: Gareth Edwards
Actors: Aaron Taylor-Johnson, Bryan Cranston, and Elizabeth Olsen

# GLOSSARY

**ATOLL** An island that is made of coral and shaped like a ring.

**CAMPY** Describing something so fake, inappropriate, or out-of-date that it is considered to be amusing.

**CAVALCADE** A series of related things.

**CONSCIOUSNESS** Knowledge that is shared by a group of people.

**DUB** To provide a film with a new soundtrack and especially dialogue in a different language.

**FALLOUT** The radioactive particles that are produced by a nuclear explosion and that fall through the atmosphere.

**GENRE** A particular type or category of literature or art.

**HAVOC** A situation in which there is much destruction or confusion.

**NOSTALGIA** Pleasure and sadness that is caused by remembering something from the past and wishing that you could experience it again.

**PROPAGANDA** Ideas or statements that are often false or exaggerated and that are spread in order to help a cause or a government.

**PSYCHOTIC** Having or relating to a very serious mental illness that makes one act strangely or believe things that are not true.

**RESTITUTION** Payment that is made to someone for damage or trouble.

**UNTRAMMELLED** Not restrained.

# FOR MORE INFORMATION

Daikaiju Enterprises Ltd. (DKE)

530 Willow Crescent

Steinbach, MB R5G 0K1

Canada

Website: http://www.g-fan.com

This is the organization behind the only journal devoted to giant movie monsters. DKE also hosts an annual convention known as G-Fest.

Legendary Pictures

4000 Warner Boulevard

Building 76

Burbank, CA 91522

(818) 954-1940

Website: http://www.legendary.com/home

This is the production studio that created the 2014 American *Godzilla*. Check out other films as well as comic books on its website.

Ottawa Comiccon

1,000,000 COMIX

1418 Pierce Street

Montreal, QC H3H 2S2

Canada

(514) 989-9587

Website: http://www.ottawacomiccon.com

The Ottawa Comiccon is a fan convention that focuses on comics, sci-fi, horror, and anime. Recently, exhibits for Godzilla fans have been added.

Toho Pictures, Inc.

1-4-1 Seijo

Setagaya-Ku, Tokyo 157-8561

Japan

Website: http://www.tohoeiga.jp/eng/aisatu.html

This is the movie studio that produced the Godzilla movies in Japan. It still holds the rights to Godzilla today.

Warner Bros. Canada

5000 Yonge Street

North York, ON M2N 6P1

Canada

(416) 250-8384

Website: http://www.warnerbroscanada.com/index.php

This is the Canadian arm of the movie company that distributed the most recent Godzilla film worldwide. See information about the making of *Godzilla* in Canada on its website.

## WEBSITES

Because of the changing nature of Internet links, Rosen Publishing has developed an online list of websites related to the subject of this book. This site is updated regularly. Please use the link to access the list:

http://www.rosenlinks.com/GMM/Godz

# FOR FURTHER READING

Borenstein, Max, Greg Borenstein, et al. *Godzilla: Awakening*. Burbank, CA: Legendary Comics, 2014.

Brothers, Peter H. *Mushroom Clouds and Mushroom Men: The Fantastic Cinema of Ishiro Honda*. Bloomington, IN: AuthorHouse, 2009.

Deamer, David. *Deleuze, Japanese Cinema, and the Atom Bomb: The Spectre of Impossibility*. New York, NY: Bloomsbury, 2014.

Greenberger, Robert. *Meet Godzilla*. New York, NY: Rosen Publishing, 2005.

Jacobs, Robert A. *Filling the Hole in the Nuclear Future: Art and Popular Culture Respond to the Bomb*. Lanham, MD: Lexington Books, 2010.

Layman, John, and Alberto Ponticelli. *Godzilla: Gangsters & Goliaths*. San Diego, CA: IDW Publishing, 2011.

McCall, Gerrie, and Chris McNab. *Movie Monsters*. New York, NY: Gareth Stevens Publishing, 2011.

Okum, David. *Manga Monster Madness: Over 50 Basic Lessons for Drawing Mutants, Robots, Dragons and More*. Avon, MA: F+W Media, 2009.

Perez, Josh, Matt Frank, et al. *Godzilla: Legends*. San Diego, CA: Idea & Design Works, 2012.

Roza, Greg. *Drawing Godzilla*. New York, NY: Windmill Books, 2011.

Vaz, Mark Cotta. *Godzilla: The Art of Destruction*. San Rafael, CA: Insight Editions, 2014.

West, Mark I. *The Japanification of Children's Popular Culture: From Godzilla to Miyazaki*. Lanham, MD: Scarecrow Press, 2009.

Westwood, Emma. *Monster Movies*. Herts, England: Pocket Essentials, 2008.

# BIBLIOGRAPHY

*American Experience.* "The 'Bravo' Test." PBS.org. Retrieved September 28, 2014 (http://www.pbs.org/wgbh/amex/bomb/peopleevents/pandeAMEX51.html).

Hibakusha Stories. "Who Are the Hibakusha?" HibakushaStories.org. Retrieved November 6, 2014 (http://www.hibakushastories.org/who-are-the-hibakusha).

Hoberman, J. "Godzilla: Poetry After the A-Bomb." The Criterion Collection, January 24, 2012. Retrieved September 30, 2014 (http://www.criterion.com/current/posts/2127-godzilla-poetry-after-the-a-bomb).

Kalat, David. *A Critical History and Filmography of Tōhō's Godzilla Series*. 2nd ed. Jefferson, NC: McFarland, 2010.

Lankes, Kevin. "Godzilla's Secret History." *Huff Post Entertainment*, April 22, 2014. Retrieved September 28, 2014 (http://www.huffingtonpost.com/kevin-lankes/godzillas-secret-history_b_5192284.html).

Leblanc, Reese. "Godzilla: Tragedy and Comedy." *Glide*, May 13, 2014. Retrieved October 15, 2014 (http://www.glidemagazine.com/117656/godzilla-tragedy-comedy).

Martin, Tim. "Godzilla: Why the Japanese Original Is No Joke." *Telegraph*, May 15, 2014. Retrieved October 2, 2014 (http://www.telegraph.co.uk/culture/film/10788996/Godzilla-why-the-Japanese-original-is-no-joke.html).

Tsui, Chris. "10 Things I Learned: *Godzilla*." The Criterion Collection, February 24, 2012. Retrieved October 5, 2014 (http://www.criterion.com/current/posts/2158-10-things-i-learned-godzilla).

Tsutsui, William. *Godzilla on My Mind: Fifty Years of the King of the Monsters*. New York, NY: Palgrave Macmillan, 2004.

Venton, Danielle. "The Impossible Anatomy of Godzilla." *Popular Mechanics*, May 16, 2014. Retrieved November 12, 2014 (http://www.popularmechanics.com/technology/digital/fact-vs-fiction/the-impossible-anatomy-of-godzilla-16785535).

Woog, Adam. *Godzilla*. Farmington Hills, MI: KidHaven Press, 2004.

# INDEX

**F**

Fukushima Daiichi nuclear plant, 28, 29–30

**G**

G-Fest, 37
*Gojira*
    ability to exist, 34
    American films, 22–23, 29–30
    creating the creature, 15–18
    critical reception, 21
    eras of films, 26–27, 28
    as *Godzilla*, 22–23
    movies inspired by, 32–33
    in other media, 33, 35–37
    plot, 9–11, 18–21
    sex of, 18

**H**

*hibakusha*, 9
Honda, Ishiro, 14–15, 18

**K**

*King Kong vs. Godzilla*, 25

**L**

*Lucky Dragon* incident, 78

**M**

monsters
    history of movie, 6–7
    other *kaiju* in Japanese films, 23–24

**N**

nuclear testing and weapons, 7–9, 10, 13, 21, 28, 29–30, 39

**S**

suitmation, 17

**T**

Tanaka, Tomoyuki, 12, 18
Tsuburaya, Eiji, 13–14, 15–18

## ABOUT THE AUTHOR

Therese Shea, an author and former educator, has written over one hundred books for children and young adults on a variety of topics, including supernatural subjects such as witchcraft and cryptozoology, as well as science fiction topics such as UFOs and aliens. She holds English and education degrees from Providence College and the State University of New York at Buffalo. The author currently resides in Rochester, New York, with her husband, Mark.

## PHOTO CREDITS

Cover (monster) © Alfo Co. Ltd/Alamy; cover (background) prudkov/Shutterstock.com; p. 5 Embassy Pictures/Moviepix/Getty Images; p. 7 The Asahi Shimbun/Getty Images; p. 10 Print Collector/Hulton Archive/Getty Images; pp. 13, 14, 16 Photofest; p. 20 Movie Poster Image Art/Moviepix/Getty Images; pp. 24, 25 © Ronald Grant Archive/Alamy; p. 28 DigitalGlobe/Getty Images; p. 30 © Warner Bros. Pictures/courtesy Everett Collection; p. 32 © Moviestore collection Ltd/Alamy; p. 34 Elena Duvernay/Stocktrek Images/Getty Images; p. 36 Koichi Kamoshida/Liason/Hulton Archive/Getty Images; p. 38 Tim Mosenfelder/Getty Images; 40–41 Andrey_Kuzmin/Shutterstock.com; interior pages banners and backgrounds Nik Merkulov/Shutterstock.com, Apostrophe/Shutterstock.com.

Designer: Brian Garvey; Editor: Shalini Saxena

JUN 2 2 2016